MW00955568

This Notebook belongs to

SCAN ME TO REORDER

Made in United States
Orlando, FL
26 November 2024

54485444R00061